THANKS for the FEEDBACK...
(I Think!)

Activity Guide for Teachers

Julia Cook

BOYS TOWN Press

Boys Town, Nebraska

Thanks for the Feedback ... (I Think!) Activity Guide for Teachers
Text and Illustrations Copyright © 2013 by Father Flanagan's Boys' Home

ISBN 978-1-934490-51-8

Published by Boys Town Press
13603 Flanagan Blvd.
Boys Town, Nebraska 68010

TO ACCESS REPRODUCIBLE FORMS – The activity handouts are available to download and can be reproduced without special permission for use in individual classrooms. To access the reproducible forms, visit BoysTownPress.org and order item number DAF-55-027. Use discount code AGTFB to download for free.

GO TO: BoysTownPress.org
ORDER: DAF-55-027
DISCOUNT CODE: AGTFB

Cover and Inside Page Design: Anne Hughes

Printed in the United States
10 9 8 7 6 5 4

For a Boys Town Press catalog, call 1-800-282-6657
or visit our website: BoysTownPress.org

What's in a Compliment?

Materials Needed

- Craft sticks (one per child)
- Jar or container to hold craft sticks
- "What's in a Compliment?" worksheet (see next page or CD)
- Pencils
- Marker

Teacher Instructions

1. Write the names of each student on a craft stick (one name per stick), and place them in the jar or container.

2. Have each child draw a stick out of the jar. Have the child write the name that is on the stick at the top of the "What's in a Compliment" worksheet.

3. Using the letters of the word "compliment," have the children fill out their sheets by writing compliments about the person whose name they drew.

4. Have all students read their compliments aloud and practice saying "Thank you" for the compliments.

Example:

C – can be a really good friend

O – on time

M – makes other people laugh

P – pretty

NOTE: Teachers can participate in this activity too!

NAME _____

what's in a Compliment?

Name of the person you drew

C - *cares about animals*
_____

O - _____

M - _____

P - _____

L - *likes to share*
_____

I - _____

M - _____

E - _____

N - *neat*
_____

T - _____

Picture "ME!"

OBJECTIVE
Students will have a positive visual image of what others think and say about them.

Materials Needed

- Dry erase board or chalkboard
- Markers or chalk
- Camera
- Printer

Teacher Instructions

1. Have a child stand in front of the marker board. (Make sure each child gets a turn in front of the board.*)

2. Ask the other students to shout out compliments about the child who is standing.

3. Neatly write down the students' compliments on the board.

4. Take a picture of the child standing under all of the compliments.

5. Print the picture and display on the classroom bulletin board.

6. Give each child/parent a copy of the child's photo.

Sam you always cheer me up!
Great smile!
You are good at math.
Positive attitude!
Cool shoes!

ALTERNATIVE   * If you have students in your room who are likely to be uncomfortable in front of the group, or if there are students who might shout out unpleasant things about a student, have them write their compliments down and then read them aloud. (Be sure to promptly and privately address any students who choose to make negative comments about someone.)

"Help Me Become a Better ME!"

OBJECTIVE

Students will understand why receiving feedback is useful, and they will learn how to give constructive, effective feedback.

NOTE: Teachers can participate in this activity too!

Materials Needed

- 🐢 "Better Me: Feedback to Grow" worksheet (on CD)
- 🐢 "Better Me: Four Squares" worksheet (see next page or CD)
- 🐢 Pencils or pens

Teacher Instructions

1. Begin by defining "feedback" as information someone can use to improve. You might say, "We all want to be the best that we can be. Sometimes, the people around us can offer really good information that can help us grow and get better. This activity will show you how to HELP each other, not HURT each other. Oftentimes, feedback is hard to hear, but if the feedback can help you grow, it's worth it!"

2. Pass out the "Better Me: Feedback to Grow" worksheet. Instruct students to write down the names of their classmates on the left side of the sheet. To the right of each classmate's name, they should write down one or two ideas (feedback) that can help that classmate grow (improve). Offer examples, such as, "Raise your hand when you want to talk so you don't interrupt so much," "Keep trying hard in math; you will get it," "Don't give up so easily," or "Try not to be a sore loser." (Students SHOULD NOT write their names on their worksheets or share their answers with others. Remind them to write down suggestions that will help someone grow.)

3. Collect all of the worksheets and confidentially compile the feedback written about each student. Reword or delete any inappropriate/hurtful/unnecessary comments. Feedback should be positive and constructive. (If you see hurtful feedback, be sure to review with the class the difference between helpful and hurtful feedback. Some may not fully understand constructive feedback, or someone may have wanted to be mean. Either way, it should be addressed.)

4. Give each student all of the feedback you recorded about him/her.

5. Hand out the "Better Me: Four Squares" worksheet. Instruct students to put the feedback they received in the appropriate square. For example, "Try not to be a sore loser at recess" would go in the "How I Act" square, and "Don't tap your pencil on your desk" would go in the "What I Do" square.

6. Review the students' worksheets individually.

7. **Optional:** Ask for volunteers to share their "Four Squares" worksheets with the class and talk about what they learned from their peers' feedback. (Use your one-on-one time with students to prepare them for group sharing and remind them to keep comments positive.)

Keep trying hard in math; you will get it.

Don't give up so easily.

Try not to be a sore loser at recess.

Better Me: Four Squares

HOW I ACT

Don't be a sore loser at recess

_____

_____

_____

_____

_____

_____

WHAT I SAY

Try not to say mean words

_____

_____

_____

_____

_____

_____

HOW OTHERS SEE ME

Don't look so mad all the time

_____

_____

_____

_____

_____

WHAT I DO

Don't tap your pencil on your desk

_____

_____

_____

_____

_____

_____

GIVE "10!"

OBJECTIVE
Through practice, students will be better at giving genuine compliments.

Materials Needed

🦕 "Give 10" worksheet (see below or CD)   🦕 Pencils or pens

Teacher Instructions

1. Instruct students to give ten people ten different compliments.

2. Hand out the "Give 10" worksheet. Have students record their compliments and the responses from the ten individuals.

3. Ask students to circle their favorite response and share it with the class.

NAME OF PERSON	COMPLIMENT GIVEN	PERSON'S RESPONSE
1.	★	★
2.	★	★
3.	★	★
4.	★	★
5.	★	★
6.	★	★
7.	★	★
8.	★	★
9.	★	★
10.	★	★

"Student of the Week" Silhouette

OBJECTIVE
Students will have posters of themselves featuring compliments from their peers.

Materials Needed

- Roll of bulletin board paper
- Scissors
- Pencil
- Markers

NOTE: Teachers can participate in this activity too!

Teacher Instructions

1. Select a "Student of the Week" and have that student lay down on bulletin board paper, posing any way he/she chooses. (Make sure each child has a turn as "Student of the Week.")

2. Trace around the student and cut out the silhouette.

3. Collect compliments about the student from classmates, either verbally as a group or individually in writing.

4. Write all of the compliments neatly onto the silhouette.

5. Hang the silhouette on your classroom wall until all students' silhouettes are hung.

Cool backpack!

Good soccer kicker!

Really good at math.

Awesome!

Neat, colorful shoes!

A Penny for Your Thoughts!

Materials Needed

 Large change jar or container   Pennies

Teacher Instructions

1. Place a "Compliment Jar" at the front of the classroom.

2. Explain to students that they can drop a penny in the jar whenever they give a sincere compliment to a classmate. (Another option is for you to manage the compliment jar by dropping a penny in whenever you hear a student complimenting others. Be sure to let a student know what he/she said that earned a penny for the jar. You could even let the student drop the penny in the jar as a reward.)

3. Practice compliments by giving each student a penny and then instructing him/her to give a sincere compliment to another classmate. After students give their compliments, have them drop their pennies in the jar. (Don't leave anyone out. Make sure all students receive at least one compliment.)

4. Practice accepting compliments appropriately by having students respond to compliments with a verbal "Thank you." (This also can be an opportunity for students to put another penny in the jar.)

5. For every penny that goes into the jar, match it. (If you hear an amazing compliment, consider adding 2 or 3 pennies.)

6. At the end of the year, use the pennies collected in the jar to help fund a class party or make a donation to charity. The students could research local charities and discuss them and choose one.

COMPLIMENT PENNIES

TEACHER NOTE This could be a blended learning opportunity for practicing addition/subtraction or counting money for younger students. "I just added 3 pennies, now how much is in there?" or "Wow, that makes 5 pennies, what is that equal to? How many more pennies do we need to equal a dime?"

Compli-ME-nt

OBJECTIVE

Students will have a better understanding of how compliments can affect others by remembering how they felt after receiving compliments.

Materials Needed

- "Compli-ME-nt" worksheet (see below or CD)
- Pens, pencils, markers, or crayons

TEACHER NOTE: If you use journaling in your class for writing practice or other activities, this would be a good topic to have a student reflect on and write about in a positive way.

Teacher Instructions

1. Pass out copies of the "Compli-ME-nt" worksheet and have students complete the worksheet independently. When students are finished, ask for volunteers to share their answers aloud and discuss as a group.

1. What was the best compliment you have ever been given?_____

   _____

2. How did it make you feel inside?_____

   _____

3. Draw a picture of how you felt when you heard the compliment.

4. What did you say back to the person?_____

   _____

5. Thinking back, should you have responded differently? Why?_____

   _____

Stand UP, Sit-DOWN, Thank You!

OBJECTIVE
Students will be able to effectively give and receive compliments.

Teacher Instructions

1. Have a student stand up, look at the classmate sitting to his/her right (or left), give the classmate a sincere compliment, and then sit down.

2. Have the student who received the compliment stand up, look at the person who complimented him/her, and say, "Thank you." Then have the student compliment the person to his/her right (or left).

3. Continue the process until every student has given and received a compliment.

4. Compliments can only be used once, so remind students to listen carefully.

5. **Optional:** After the activity, ask students to share with the group which compliments they liked best.

Let's Feed the Feedback Box!

OBJECTIVE

Student will have a safe way to compliment others and offer other general suggestions for making improvements.

Materials Needed

- Shoebox or other container with an opening, as shown
- Paper slips
- Pencils

Teacher Instructions

1. Start by explaining to your students that feedback is information to help them grow and improve.

2. Tell students that if they have suggestions on how to make the classroom better, make instructional time more effective, or improve their school experience, they can write down their suggestions and put them in the Feedback Box. (Other teachers and staff can participate, too.) Also, if they want to give others compliments, they can write their compliments on paper and put them in the box.

3. Once a week, empty the box, review the comments (discarding any that are inappropriate), and then choose a student to read aloud the remaining suggestions and compliments to the class.

NOTE When offering feedback suggestions, remind students to keep them general (or broad) so every student can benefit from them. Here is an example to share: If a student always whistles during work time and is distracting, don't write, "Jonathan, STOP whistling." Instead, write a more general statement, such as, "We need to be as quiet as we can when it's work time so we don't distract others."

It's imperative for you to read the feedback suggestions first and translate them into useful information so no child is hurt by harsh or inappropriate comments.

The Fruit Snack Critic

OBJECTIVE
Students will be better able to give constructive feedback.

Materials Needed

- Five different types of fruit snacks
- "Fruit Snack Critic" worksheet (see next page or CD)
- Pencils or pens
- Small paper plates

TEACHER NOTE: This is a great opportunity to have students practice writing business letters.

Teacher Instructions

1. Divide students into groups of four, have each group sample the five types of fruit snacks, and then have the group members discuss their opinions with each other.

2. Hand out copies of the "Fruit Snack Critic" worksheet, and instruct students to read and answer the questions.

3. Ask each student to share his/her answers with the class.

4. Have students email or write a letter to the fruit snack manufacturer, telling the company what they think.

TEACHER NOTE You can also have kids read food reviews in a local newspaper or online.

14

Fruit Snack Critic

Name of Fruit Snack: _____

Name and Contact of Manufacturer: _____

List three things that you like about this fruit snack:

1. _____

2. _____

3. _____

List three ways that the manufacturer could make this fruit snack more appealing to kids:

1. _____

_____

2. _____

_____

3. _____

_____

KEEPER or PITCHER?
Steps to Becoming a Better "ME!"

> ### OBJECTIVE
> Students will know the difference between "Keeper Feedback" (helpful information they can use to grow and improve) and "Pitcher Feedback" (hurtful information they can ignore).

Materials Needed

- Footprints cut out of construction paper (at least two per student, on CD)
- Strips of scratch paper (two per student)
- Dry erase board or chalkboard
- Markers
- Garbage can
- Bulletin board

Teacher Instructions

1. Begin by defining "Keeper Feedback" as information that helps someone ("You should never text and drive!") and "Pitcher Feedback" as information that hurts someone's feelings ("You're stupid!").

2. Ask students to give you two examples of feedback they have received (both positive and negative). Make sure all of the students participate, and record their responses on the board.

3. Give each student two strips of paper and two footprints. Have them choose two examples from the board and write each one on separate paper strips. (All comments on the board should be used. Avoid having everyone choose the same comments.)

4. Have students take turns reading their strips aloud. As a group, decide if a comment is a "Keeper" or a "Pitcher." If a comment is a "Keeper," have the student copy it neatly on a footprint. If a comment is a "Pitcher," have the student wad the paper strip into a ball and toss it into the trash can. (You also can have students tear them into tiny pieces, throw the pieces on the floor, sweep them into a dust pan, and toss them into the trash!)

5. Lead a discussion about the differences between "Keeper Feedback" and "Pitcher Feedback."

6. Collect all of the footprints and use them to decorate your bulletin board under the headline, "Steps to Becoming a Better ME!"

7. Wrap up the activity by reminding students that they will receive many forms of feedback inside and outside the classroom. If the feedback is a "Keeper," they should find ways to use it. If the feedback is a "Pitcher," they should find ways to ignore it.

...e!

...nderstanding of how to give and receive feedback.

> **TEACHER NOTE:**
> For more advanced students, you could adapt this activity for a lesson on current events or civics. Have students observe a nightly newscast or a televised debate, and then script some examples of the kind of feedback they would offer.

...sheet

...lity TV Time" worksheet.

...ty program (*The Voice*, ...ce, *Top Chef*, etc.) where contestants receive feedback.

...nstruct students to fill out their "Reality TV Time" ..., have volunteers share their answers aloud.

4. Lead a class ... examples from the TV show that highlight good and bad ways of giving and receiving feedback.

NAME _____

Reality TV Time

Act 1: _____ Date: _____

Name(s) of performer(s)/group: _____

1. Write a brief description of what you saw. _____

_____

_____

2. What did the judges say? (Include both positive and negative feedback.) _____

_____

_____

3. Do you think the feedback that the judges gave was helpful to the performer(s)? Why or why not?

_____

_____

4. How did the contestant(s) respond when the feedback was given?_____

_____

_____

5. What feedback would you have given? _____

_____

_____

6. What has this activity taught you about giving and receiving feedback? _____

_____

_____

Stand Up, Sit Down - I LIKE, but I'd LOVE!

OBJECTIVE
Students will know how to offer positive compliments and constructive feedback.

Teacher Instructions

1. Have a student stand up, look at the classmate sitting to his/her right (or left), and say, "I really like it when you *[name an activity or personal quality]*, but I would LOVE it if you would *[name a different activity or personal quality]*."

2. Have the student who received the compliment and suggestion stand up, look at the person who complimented him/her, and say, "Thank you." Then have the student give a compliment and suggestion to the person to his/her right (or left).

3. Continue the process until every student has given and received a compliment and suggestion.

4. Compliments and suggestions can only be used once, so remind students to listen carefully.

5. **Optional:** After the activity, ask students to share with the group which compliments and suggestions they liked best.

Thank you.

I really LIKE it when you know the answer to a question, but I would LOVE it if you would raise your hand first.

I really LIKE it when you smile, but I would LOVE it if you would show your teeth when you smile.

Thank you!

Thanks!

Thank you.

I really LIKE it when you finish your homework, but I would LOVE it if you wouldn't rush it.

Design a T-Shirt

OBJECTIVE

Students will show their creativity by making a visual reminder of why feedback is important.

Materials Needed

- T-Shirt pattern
- Markers and/or color pencils

Teacher Instructions

1. Hand out copies of the T-shirt pattern available on the CD.

2. Instruct students to design a T-shirt with the theme "Feedback is just information that is HELPING ME GROW!"

3. Display their designs on the bulletin board.

What People are Saying about "_____"
-- Consumer Reports

OBJECTIVE
Students will be able to evaluate feedback given by consumers and decide if it is helpful or not.

Materials Needed

- Internet access
- "Consumer Feedback" worksheet (see next page or CD)
- Pencils or pens

Teacher Instructions

1. Have students research a product of their choice online, and read what consumers and others have written about it. For example, what do people say about your favorite author's books? What car gets the best gas mileage? Which crayons last the longest? Which video games do kids prefer? Where is the best place to buy video games? Who makes the best baseball bats for kids? What longboard is the best?

2. Instruct students to read consumer comments and opinions about their chosen product.

3. Hand out copies of the "Consumer Feedback" worksheet, and give students enough time to complete the worksheet independently.

4. When students finish, have them share and explain their answers aloud.

TEACHER NOTE This is a great opportunity to incorporate teaching around concepts such as consumerism, truth in advertising, and even supply and demand.

Consumer Feedback

My product: _____

Before doing this activity, my opinion about this product is: _____

_____

1. Here is a list of what people said (opinions – list both positive and negative): _____

    _____

    _____

2. The research said: _____

    _____

    _____

3. Was all of the feedback you read about your product helpful? Why or why not?

    _____

    _____

4. After completing this activity, your opinion about the product has (choose a or b)...

    a. changed because: _____

    b. stayed the same because: _____

5. Feedback is information that helps you grow. How did researching feedback about your product

    help you grow? _____

    _____

6. Why is it easier to listen to feedback about an item or product than it is to hear feedback about

    yourself? _____

    _____

Tell Me about IT!

Materials Needed

- "Interview Questions" worksheet (see below or CD)
- Pencils or pens

Teacher Instructions

1. Give each student multiple copies of the "Interview Questions" worksheet. The questions are:
   a. What was one of the best compliments you have ever gotten?
   b. How did it make you feel inside?
   c. Who gave you the compliment?
   d. What did you say back to the person?
   e. What was the most valuable feedback you have ever gotten from a person?
   f. Was it negative or positive?
   g. Why was it valuable to you?
   h. Did it change you in any way?
   i. When people give you negative feedback, how does it make you feel?
   j. When people give you negative feedback, how do you react?

2. Instruct students to interview five to ten different people, asking them the questions written on the worksheet. Students should record the responses on the worksheets.

3. When students complete their interviews, have them review the responses and use percentages (if possible) to quantify the answers. (For example, 70% said the best compliment they ever received made them feel "awesome," or 100% said compliments changed their behaviors.)

4. Have students share their interviews with the class.

5. Lead a class discussion by asking students if they were surprised by anything they heard, and what did they learn from the experience.

Climbing Up the Feedback Success Ladder

OBJECTIVE
Students will learn the behavioral steps to accepting feedback appropriately.

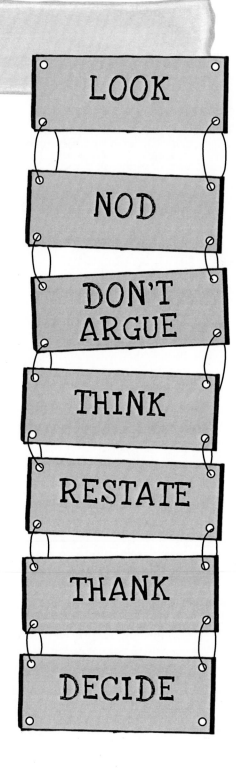

Materials Needed

- Ladder diagram for bulletin board
- Strips or rectangular pieces of poster board (that look like steps)
- Markers

Teacher Instructions

1. Copy the following behavioral steps on the poster board, and then explain each step to the class.

   - *Look at the person, and say his/her name.*
   - *Agree to what is said by nodding and saying, "Okay."*
   - *Don't argue.*
   - *Think about the other person's point of view.*
   - *Restate what the person said in a positive way. "I will try harder to…."*
   - *Thank the person. "Thanks for talking with me and letting me know."*
   - *Decide if the information is a KEEPER or a PITCHER.*

Shortened version: Look, Nod, Don't Argue, Think, Restate, Thank, Decide

Easier Said than Done!

OBJECTIVE
Students will be better able to accept feedback.

Materials Needed

- Feedback Success Ladder (see previous activity)
- "Rubric Role-Play Review" worksheet (see next page or CD)
- Pencils or pens

Teacher Instructions

1. As a group, have students brainstorm situations where they might receive positive and negative feedback.

2. Tell students that accepting feedback is a helpful skill and is a way for them to show others that they are willing to hear new ideas and points of view, and feedback is just information that can help them grow.

3. Hand out copies of the "Rubric Role-Play Review" worksheet.

4. Group students in pairs and have each group role-play giving and accepting feedback using a scenario from the brainstorming session. (Remind students that feedback should be helpful, not hurtful.)

5. After each pair role-plays in front of the class, have students fill out a worksheet. When they're finished, ask for volunteers to share their answers with the class.

6. Have an ongoing discussion during the activity about the importance of being able to accept feedback from others.

NAME _____

Rubric Role-Play Review

Did the student look at the person and use his/her name?   Yes   No

Did the student say "Okay" even if he/she didn't agree at the time?   Yes   No

Did the student argue with the person?   Yes   No

Did the student think about what the person said and why?   Yes   No

Did the student restate what was said in a positive manner?   Yes   No

Did the student thank the person for talking with him/her?   Yes   No

Did the student decide to KEEP or PITCH the information?   KEEP   PITCH

Masterpiece Feedback

OBJECTIVE
Students will be able to give and receive compliments and feedback.

Materials Needed

- 🦕 "Feedback Masterpiece 1," "Feedback Masterpiece 2," and "Feedback Masterpiece 3" (on CD)
- 🦕 Markers, crayons, or color pencils
- 🦕 Lined notebook paper

Teacher Instructions

1. Show students the black and white versions of "Feedback Masterpiece 1," "Feedback Masterpiece 2," and "Feedback Masterpiece 3," and let them choose which one they would like to color.

2. Have students fold their chosen masterpiece page in half and then color one side. They can color the half-page like it appears in the *Feedback* book, or they can color it completely different.

3. When students finish, tape their half-completed masterpieces on a wall. (It may be helpful to only tape five at a time.)

4. Ask students to look at the posted masterpieces and give compliments aloud about each one. The student whose masterpiece is being complimented should record the compliments on a notepaper.

5. When students finish with their compliments, have them offer feedback on how a masterpiece can be improved. The student whose masterpiece is being critiqued should record the feedback on a notepaper.

6. When all students have recorded compliments and feedback about their masterpiece, have them review their notes. Instruct students to use the feedback to color the other half of their masterpiece so it is the BEST it can be!

7. Wrap up the activity by asking students whether or not they found the feedback useful.

The Feedback Sculpture

OBJECTIVE

Students will build a "Feedback Sculpture" by giving genuine compliments and offering constructive feedback to their peers.

Materials Needed

- Mini marshmallows
- Toothpicks
- Flat work area

Teacher Instructions

1. Using marshmallows and toothpicks, create a base for a structure (as shown on the right).

2. Each time a student gives a genuine compliment or feedback, give that student a mini marshmallow and a toothpick. Have the student add to the structure.

3. Each week take a picture of the built structure, then tear it down and start again.

4. Display the pictures on a bulletin board.

5. Discuss the importance of giving and receiving compliments and feedback with your students throughout the activity.

6. **Optional:** Leave the structure and just add to it each week.

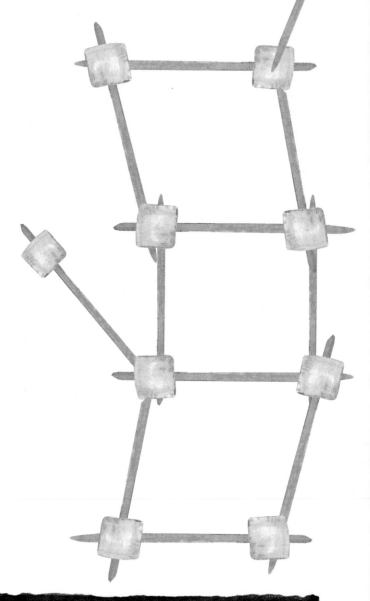

TEACHER NOTE You could incorporate math and geometry lessons. Have students begin by creating simple polygons with their toothpicks and marshmallows, then expand the activity over time into more advanced shapes. It's also a great way to demonstrate concepts such as how to calculate area or volume.

The Feedback Balance

OBJECTIVE
Students will understand the importance of having a feedback balance.

Materials Needed

- "Imagine a Life Where..." worksheet (see below or CD)
- Pencils or pens

Teacher Instructions

1. Hand out copies of the "Imagine a Life Where..." worksheet, have students complete the worksheet, then discuss their answers as a group.

Imagine a Life Where...

Nobody EVER gave you feedback or a compliment!

1. What would your life be like?

2. How would your life be different?

3. Draw a picture of what you would look like.

Everyone gave you feedback and compliments CONSTANTLY!

1. What would your life be like?

2. How would your life be different?

3. Draw a picture of what you would look like.

4. What advice can you offer others when it comes to feedback?

It is so important to have a compliment and feedback balance in our lives. That balance is unique to every person. Why do you think that is?

It's Complimentary!

OBJECTIVE

Students will know how and when to give a compliment.

Materials Needed

🦕 "Tips for Giving Compliments" handout (see below or CD)

Teacher Instructions

1. Pass out copies of the "Tips for Giving Compliments" handout.

2. As a class, review and discuss each tip.

Tips for Giving Compliments

Choose a genuine, specific thing to compliment the person about.
("You have a great smile!")

Personalize your compliment. *("You make that hat look amazing!")*

Make eye contact with the person you are complimenting.
Eye contact will show that you are sincere.

When you see something to praise, give your compliment right away. When others are around, make sure they hear it. *(If you are complimenting your mom for making a great meal, say it during the meal and in front of the rest of the family so everyone can hear it.)*

Avoid compliments that use a comparison or value statement.
(Instead of saying, "You look a lot better than I do," say, "You look great!")

Change your compliments around and reword them so they don't always sound the same. *("I really love your laugh," or "Your laugh just made my day!")*

If your compliment is taken the wrong way or is not accepted *(The person rolls his/her eyes at you, etc.),* **don't try to correct the situation, just move on.**

Rap It Up!

Materials Needed

- Social skill poems (see below or CD)
- Notepaper
- Pencils or pens

Teacher Instructions

1. Divide students into groups of three or four.

2. Using the information in the poems below, have each group create a song or rap. (Words can be rearranged.)

3. Have each group perform its song/rap for the class.

COMPLIMENT

When somebody gives you a compliment,
The best thing for you to do,
Is to look at the person, use a nice, pleasant voice,
And simply say, "Thank You!"

FEEDBACK

When somebody gives you feedback,
He/She is helping to improve who you are.
Listen to the person, and say, "OK."
The words just might take you far.
Make sure that you remember to always look
At the one who is talking to you.
Stay calm on the inside, no matter what is said,
Then carefully think it through.

Accepting Positive and Negative Feedback Appropriately

Materials Needed

- **Reward coupon** (see below or CD)

Teacher Instructions

1. Observe students during their interactions with you and others. Pay close attention to the way they accept positive (compliments) and negative (criticism) feedback.

Suggested rewards for earning coupons:

- Put a marble in the marble jar.
- Go to the front of the line.
- Sit in the teacher's chair for an hour.

- Be the official daily message runner.
- Help pass out worksheets/notes for a day.
- Have lunch with the teacher one day.

Dear _____, **WOW!**

Today you _____

_____!

You have earned _____!

Nice Job!

SIGNED _____ DATE _____